ISBN 978-0-260-00649-3
PIBN 10921719

This book is a reproduction of an important historical work. Forgotten Books uses
state-of-the-art technology to digitally reconstruct the work, preserving the original format
whilst repairing imperfections present in the aged copy. In rare cases, an imperfection in
the original, such as a blemish or missing page, may be replicated in our edition. We do,
however, repair the vast majority of imperfections successfully; any imperfections that
remain are intentionally left to preserve the state of such historical works.

...torical Microreproductions / Institut canadien de microreproductions historiques

1998

graphic Notes / Notes techniques et bibliographiques

in the best original
of this copy which
ch may alter any of
n, or which may
thod of filming are

L'Institut a microfilmé le meilleur exemplaire qu'il lui a
été possible de se procurer. Les détails de cet exemplaire qui sont peut-être uniques du point de vue bibli-
ographique, qui peuvent modifier une image reproduite,
ou qui peuvent exiger une modification dans la méthode normale de filmage sont indiqués ci-dessous.

☐ Coloured pages / Pages de couleur

☐ Pages damaged / Pages endommagées

☐ Pages restored and/or laminated /
Pages restaurées et/ou pelliculées

ed /
iculée

☑ Pages discoloured, stained or foxed /
Pages décolorées, tachetées ou piquées

couverture manque

☐ Pages detached / Pages détachées

phiques en couleur

☑ Showthrough / Transparence

e or black) /
bleue ou noire)

☐ Quality of print varies /
Qualité inégale de l'impression

ons /
ouleur

☐ Includes supplementary material /
Comprend du matériel supplémentaire

☐ Pages wholly or partially obscured by errata slips,
tissues, etc., have been refilmed to ensure the best
possible image / Les pages totalement ou
partiellement obscurcies par un feuillet d'errata, une
pelure, etc., ont été filmées à nouveau de façon à
s or distortion along
ée peut causer de
long de la marge
obtenir la meilleure image possible.

☐ Opposing pages with varying colouration or
discolourations are filmed twice to ensure the best
possible image / Les pages s'opposant ayant des
rations may appear
le, these have been
ue certaines pages
ine restauration
, lorsque cela était
é filmées.
colorations variables ou des décolorations sont
filmées deux fois afin d'obtenir la meilleure image
possible.

The copy filmed here has been reproduced thanks to the generosity of:

National Library of Canada

The images appearing here are the best quality possible considering the condition and legibility of the original copy and in keeping with the filming contract specifications.

Original copies in printed paper covers are filmed beginning with the front cover and ending on the last page with a printed or illustrated impression, or the back cover when appropriate. All other original copies are filmed beginning on the first page with a printed or illustrated impression, and ending on the last page with a printed or illustrated impression.

The last recorded frame on each microfiche shall contain the symbol ➡ (meaning "CONTINUED"), or the symbol ▽ (meaning "END"), whichever applies.

Maps, plates, charts, etc., may be filmed at different reduction ratios. Those too large to be entirely included in one exposure are filmed beginning in the upper left hand corner, left to right and top to bottom, as many frames as required. The following diagrams illustrate the method:

1   2   3

L'exemplaire filmé fut reproduit grâce à la générosité de:

Bibliothèque nationale du Canada

Les images suivantes ont été reproduites avec le plus grand soin, compte tenu de la condition et de la netteté de l'exemplaire filmé, et en conformité avec les conditions du contrat de filmage.

Les exemplaires originaux dont la couverture en papier est imprimée sont filmés en commençant par le premier plat et en terminant soit par la dernière page qui comporte une empreinte d'impression ou d'illustration, soit par le second plat, selon le cas. Tous les autres exemplaires originaux sont filmés en commençant par la première page qui comporte une empreinte d'impression ou d'illustration et en terminant par la dernière page qui comporte une telle empreinte.

Un des symboles suivants apparaitra sur la dernière image de chaque microfiche, selon le cas: le symbole ➡ signifie "A SUIVRE", le symbole ▼ signifie "FIN".

Les cartes, planches, tableaux, etc., peuvent être filmés à des taux de réduction différents. Lorsque le document est trop grand pour être reproduit en un seul cliché, il est filmé à partir de l'angle supérieur gauche, de gauche à droite, et de haut en bas, en prenant le nombre d'images nécessaire. Les diagrammes suivants illustrent la méthode.

1

2

MICROCOPY RESOLUTION TEST CHART

(ANSI and ISO TEST CHART No. 2)

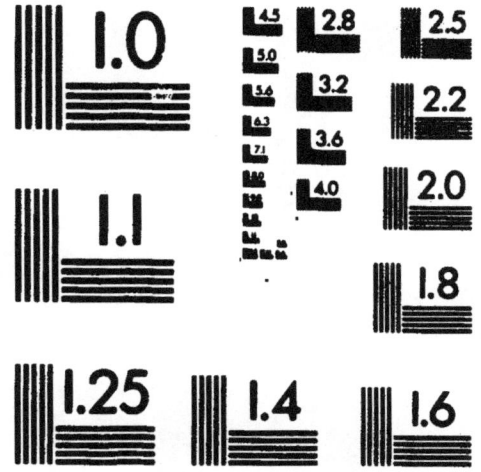

APPLIED IMAGE Inc

1653 East Main Street
Rochester, New York   14609   USA
(716) 482 – 0300 – Phone
(716) 288 – 5989 – Fax

Constitution and By-Laws

OF

The United Farmers of Ontario

Our Motto

"EQUAL OPPORTUNITIES FOR ALL"

1914
(162)

CONSTITUTION AND BY-LAWS

OF

The United Farmers of Ontario

Our Motto: "Equal Opportunities for All"

NAME

1. This Association shall be called The United Farmers of Ontario.

OBJECTS

2. The objects of this Association shall be to further the interests of farmers in all branches of agriculture.

(a) By fostering mutual understanding.

(b) By encouraging the study of farm and household questions so as to increase the efficiency and comfort of the farmer and his family.

(c) By promoting social intercourse and the study of economic and social questions through the holding of debates and lectures, the dessemination of literature, the establishment of libraries, and so forth; and by otherwise extending the knowledge of mem bers and their families, with the view of elevating the standard of living in rural communities.

(d) By watching legislation relating to the farmers' interests, and by urging from time to time through duly appointed delegates or otherwise, the passing of legislation required to promote the best interests of Agriculture.

(e) By studying and teaching the principles of co-operation, and by promoting the establishment of co-operative organizations.

(f) By encouraging members to provide suitable halls or meeting places and properly furnish and equip the same for the social and educational benefit of the members.

(g) By endeavoring to suppress personal, local, sectional, national and class prejudices, and thereby to promote the best interests of Canada as a whole.

THE CENTRAL ASSOCIATION

3. The Central Association shall consist of all duly admitted and fully paid up members of Branch Associations.

4. The Central Association shall be governed by the Annual Convention, composed of delegates from each branch not in arrears to the Association, elected thus:—One delegate for each branch, and an additional delegate for every twenty, or major portion of twenty, over the first twenty members. All delegates shall be appointed annually.

5. The Annual Convention of the Central Association shall be held at such place and on such date between December 1st and March 1st as shall be fixed by the board of Directors.

6. The business of the Annual Convention shall be:—

(a) To receive and discuss the reports of the Executive officers and Board of Directors, and to decide on any question arising out of such reports. All reports shall be furnished to the Branch Associations not later than one month prior to the opening of the convention, and shall contain a detailed statement of receipts and ex.enditures, assets and liabilities.

(b) To elect by ballot from duly accredited delegates present at the convention the officers and auditors for the ensuing year.

(c) To decide on any new business brought before the convention by the Board of Directors or by any Branch Association in good standing.

(d) Special Conventions may be called by the Board of Directors through the Secretary, by giving at least two weeks notice to each Branch Association, such notice to state the business for which the convention is called and no other business to be allowed to be introduced.

(e) No voting by proxy shall be allowed in any convention.

(f) The railway fare of all duly qualified delegates to annual or special conventions shall be borne by the Central Association.

OFFICERS

7. The officers of the Central Association shall include a president, first and second vice presidents, a secretary-treasurer, five directors, and two auditors. The President, Vice-Presidents, Directors and Auditors shall be nominated and elected by ballot or standing vote by the whole assembly. The Secretary-Treasurer shall be appointed by the Board of Directors who shall fix his remuneration, and he shall hold office at the pleasure of the Board. All officers shall hold office until their successors are appointed.

8. The Executive of the Central Association shall consist of the President, Secretary, Treasurer and three Vice-Presidents or Directors of the Association, elected by the Board.

9. The Executive of the Central Association shall hold a meeting or meetings, each year, on such date or dates as the President may decide, or at the instance of any three of the Executive. Due notice of all meetings must be given.

DUTIES OF OFFICERS

10. It shall be the duty of the President to preside at all meetings of the Association, decide all questions of order, and make any suggestions he may deem necessary in the interest of the Association.

11. The Vice-President shall assist the President in his duties when called upon, and in the President's absence he shall perform the duties of that station. In the absence of the First Vice-President his duties shall be performed by the Second Vice-President.

12. It shall be the duty of the Secretary-Treasurer to attend all meetings of the Central Association, the Officers, and the Executive, and keep correct minutes of the same as well as a complete and correct membership roll, showing date of joining, and an account of each member, showing dues and when paid, and everything necessary to keep a record of each member's standing. He shall keep all books necessary to the proper discharge of his duties and shall conduct all official correspondence, issue all press and other reports and prepare for publication the annual re-

port. As Treasurer he shall receive and account for all monies belonging to the Association, pay all bills and accounts that have been approved by the executive. By virtue of his office he shall be a member of each committee apointed and shall perform such other duties as may from time to time be required. As Treasurer he shall be required to give good and sufficient bonds in such sum as may be fixed by the executive.

13. It shall be the duty of each officer and representative to support at all times the ruling of the majority, whether at the Annual Meeting, a meeting of the officers, or an executive meeting, his opinion to the contrary notwithstanding.

14. No officer shall disclose motions, rulings, names of movers, seconders, etc., provided that the meeting rules that such data shall not be made public, nor shall any officer except the Secretary, furnish newspaper reports of meetings or proceedings.

15.. The person whose name is placed first on a committee shall be the convener of that committee.

16. In case a vacancy occurs in the officers or directors, the executive shall fill the vacancy.

QUORUM

17. Not less than twenty-five members shall be a quorum to transact business for the Central Association, not less than five shall be a quorum at any directors' meeting and not less than three members shall be a quorum at an Executive meeting.

18. At least one month's notice shall be given of each annual or general meeting, naming time and place of meeting. Notice may be given through the public press, or by circular letter mailed to each member, or to each Secretary of the Branch Associations, as the Executive may deem wise.

19. At least ten days' notice shall be given of all meetings of the Board of Directors or the Executive Committee of the Central Association, provided that an emergency meeting may be held at any time upon waiver of notice being given by all members of the Board, or Executive.

LIFE MEMBERSHIP

20. Any member may, by sending his name and address with the sum of twelve dollars ($12.00) to the central office of the Association, become a life member, but without convention privileges unless duly elected a delegate by a branch association; and such life member shall pay one half of the annual membership fee to the branch to which he belongs, in order to have standing in that branch. Two dollars of the Life Membership Fee shall go to the general revenue of the Association, and the balance shall be used for organization purposes, or invested as a reserve fund, as the Annual Convention may determine, so that the proceeds thereof shall make for the permanent establishment of the Association.

BY-LAWS

21. The Board of Directors shall frame such By-laws and regulations for its own and the Association's government as are in its

judgment for the best interests of the Association and not inconsistent with this constitution.

AMENDMENTS TO CONSTITUTION

22. Any member desiring to introduce an addition or amendment to this constitution shall submit a draft thereof to the Secretary at least thirty days prior to the date of the annual meeting, and the Secretary shall forthwith communicate the same to each local Secretary by circular letter.

23. An addition or amendment to the constitution shall require a three fifths vote of the members present and voting at the annual meeting to pass.

MEMBERSHIP

24. Any person directly interested in farming may join the Central or any Branch Association by being introduced by any member and paying the annual membership fee of not less than 50c. Each application shall be submitted at a regular meeting and shall be accepted by a majority vote of the members present to be taken in such way as may at the time be determined.

25. In every case where a married farmer becomes a member his wife and daughters shall be honorary members; sons of such farmers, if under the age of 21 years, and if living at home and working on their father's farm, shall be admitted as members on what shall be known as the family ticket at a fee of 50 per cent. of the full membership fee.

26. A member six months in arrears shall stand suspended without action of the Association, but the Secretary must report the

same to the Association and correct the membership roll. A member suspended for non-payment of dues may be reinstated by the payment of all arrears.

27. The Secretary of each branch shall report every six months to the Central Association, and shall forward with such report twenty five cents (25c) per member, and no branch shall have status at an annual or special convention of the Central Association until the membership report, together with fees due, has been forwarded.

BRANCH ASSOCIATIONS

28. A branch Association may be organized by at least ten (10) qualified persons applying to the Central or a Branch Association or organizer to be so organized, on receipt of which application the association or organizer shall proceed to effect such organization and make due report thereof to the Association; or, not less than ten persons as aforesaid may assemble of their own accord and proceed to organize themselves into an association by subscribing to this constitution, electing officers herein provided and making due report to the Central Association.

29. The Central Association recommends that the officers of a Branch Association consist of President, Vice-President, Secretary and Treasurer, or Secretary-Treasurer, and not more than six directors.

30. The executive of a branch association shall consist of the officers of the said association.

31. The official term of office in the case of branch associations shall be one year, and regular elections shall be held in November of each year.

32. Branch associations should meet at least monthly if possible, and it shall be the duty of the President, Vice-Presidents and Secretary, or such special committee as may be appointed for the purpose, to see that there is an entertaining program or subject for consideration at each meeting.

33. Branch associations shall have the power to deal with their members for offences against the association and shall be governed by rules usually applied in such cases.

34. Any subordinate Granges, Farmers Clubs, Farmers' Associations or Farmers' Unions, not organized under these rules, desiring to affiliate with the Central Association and become recognized as a branch thereof, may do so by communicating with the Central Association and agreeing to be governed by this constitution.

35. It shall be the duty of the Secretaries of all branch associations to prepare annual statements and to supply all information asked for by the general secretary before November 30th of each year.

GENERAL PROVISIONS

(1) The members of the Association are expected to extend fraternal care to one another in sickness, misfortune or distress, and to members' families in bereavement. The industrious, however, shall not be required to lightly bestow their substance upon the shiftless and improvident.

(2) Members of the Association are expected to cultivate harmonious relations with all other farmers' associations or organizations.

(3) Members should help each other in their business relations and they should never go to law over their differences until all other means of agreement and settlement are exhausted. In all such cases the association recommends arbitration.

(4) Due decorum must be observed in all the meetings, and presiding officers are given ample power to enforce order. Cushing's and Robert's manuals are given as authorities for parliamentary rules and usages.

(5) Every effort should be made to encourage young persons to take part in the exercises, and all should regard the meetings as schools of progress and advancement. The members are enjoined to faithfully attend the meetings and spare no pains to make them interesting and profitable.

(6) Co-operation is the great means by which we are to overcome the evil effects of hurtful combinations, and members are urged to avail themselves of every opportunity for profitable co-operation with each other, but we should never let this purpose breed a spirit of antagonism between legitimate local interests.

(7) Co-operative marketing is the means in our hands for compelling equitable prices for our products, and members should hold it their duty to adhere strictly to that principle, and urge that their neighbors do the same, even if not members. Adherence to this principle is a test of good membership, and all are expected to direct their best efforts thereto.

ORDER OF BUSINESS

The following order of business at all meetings of the branches is suggested as a guide:

1. Call to order by President or Chairman.

2. Call the roll of officers, noting those present. The chairman will fill vacancies.

3. Call the roll of paid up members, noting those present.

4. Reading and disposing of minutes of previous meeting.

5. Reading of all official communications received by the Secretary.

6. Call for applications for Membership.

7. Reports of Committees.

8. Unfinished business.

9. Addresses and discussions.

10. Opening of question drawer.

11. Election of officers (Annual Meeting.)

12. New business.

(1) Does any member know of a case of sickness, distress or death in the neighborhood that needs special attention?

(2) If so, appoint a special committee to take up such cases, and devise ways and means for handling same.

(3) Members wishing work.

(4) Members requiring help.

(5) Members wishing to sell anything.

(6) Members wishing to buy anything.

(7) Members wishing to report a grievance.

(8) Report on market conditions affecting the products of the neighborhood.

(9) General crop prospects of the neighborhood.

(10) Any matter for insertion in official bulletins of association.

(11) Discussion of topics for general good and welfare.

(13) Social entertainment. (It is understood that the ladies and young people are always welcome at the meetings and a special effort should be made to get them to take part in all discussions that may be arranged.)

(14) Has the regular report been forwarded to the Central Office?

(15) Adjournment.

The following are also suggested as rules for the conduct of business:—

(1) Except by permission of the presiding officer, no member or other person should speak except to ask a question or to introduce or speak to a motion.

(2) In the discussions following the introduction of a subject, no person should speak more than twice or for a longer time than five minutes, except by a vote of the meeting.

(4)   Before the vote is taken on any motion or amendment, the President should ask: "Is the meeting ready for the question?" The motion should not be put so long as any members desires to speak and is in order. Any member desirous of asking a question on the subject introduced may do so verbally; but if he desires to ask more than two questions he should submit them to the secretary in writing.

CPSIA information can be obtained
at www.ICGtesting.com
Printed in the USA
BVHW04*0957080818
523918BV00012B/188/P